**POWER
POSITIVITY**

# I AM
# AWESOME

quadrille

# BEING PROUD OF YOURSELF IS NOT ARROGANT; IT IS A SIGN OF SELF-RESPECT.

Alice Walker

YOU REALLY HAVE TO LOOK
INSIDE YOURSELF AND FIND
YOUR OWN INNER STRENGTH,
AND SAY, 'I'M PROUD OF WHAT
I AM AND WHO I AM, AND I'M
JUST GOING TO BE MYSELF.'

**Mariah Carey**

# CONFIDENCE IS YOUR BEST ACCESSORY. THERE IS NOTHING ELSE YOU NEED.

# THE ONLY THING YOU NEED TO WEAR WELL IS YOUR CONFIDENCE.

Priyanka Chopra

# I DON'T BELONG TO ANYONE ELSE BUT MYSELF.
# I HAVE TO MAKE MY OWN DECISIONS.
# HAPPINESS IS DEFINED BY ME.

**Keke Palmer**

I DON'T KNOW HOW TO BE ANYTHING BUT MYSELF. [...] PLEASE STAY TRUE TO YOURSELF. PLEASE JUST REMAIN WHO YOU ARE.

Selena Gomez

**WHATEVER FEAR
I HAVE INSIDE ME,
MY DESIRE TO WIN
IS ALWAYS STRONGER.**

**Serena Williams**

# MY RECIPE FOR LIFE IS NOT BEING AFRAID OF MYSELF, AFRAID OF WHAT I THINK OR OF MY OPINIONS.

Eartha Kitt

# I DON'T GO BY THE RULE BOOK ...

# I LEAD FROM THE HEART, NOT THE HEAD.

**Princess Diana**

# IT'S OKAY IF YOU'RE NOT PERFECT, YOU KNOW. IT'S ABOUT ACCEPTING THE BEAUTY OF IMPERFECTION.

Kendrick Lamar

I NEEDED TO LEARN
THAT THE IDEAS THAT
I HAD WERE AS GOOD AS
ANYONE ELSE'S IDEAS.

**J.J. Abrams**

WE'VE GOT TO ACT LIKE
WE BELIEVE IN OURSELVES.
BECAUSE WHEN WE BELIEVE
IN OURSELVES AND ACT ON IT,
WE CREATE POSSIBILITIES
THAT NEVER WOULD HAVE
BEEN POSSIBLE HAD WE
NOT JUST BELIEVED.

Sheryl Lee Ralph

CALL OUT EACH OTHER'S WINS, AND JUST LIKE WE DO ON THE FIELD, CLAIM THE SUCCESS OF ONE WOMAN AS A COLLECTIVE SUCCESS FOR ALL WOMEN. JOY. SUCCESS. POWER. THESE ARE NOT PIES WHERE A BIGGER SLICE FOR HER MEANS A SMALLER SLICE FOR YOU. THESE ARE INFINITE.

Abby Wambach

THERE IS POWER IN
WHAT WE DO EVERY DAY.
AND I HAVE TO REMIND
MYSELF OF THAT EVERY
SINGLE MOMENT. BUT NOW
THAT I'M OLDER, I CAN
NOW LOOK BACK AND
SAY, 'YEAH, I AM WORTHY.'

**Michelle Obama**

**YOU CAN NEVER BE THE BEST TECHNICALLY. SOMEONE WILL ALWAYS HAVE A HIGHER JUMP OR A MORE BEAUTIFUL LINE. THE ONLY THING YOU CAN BE THE BEST AT IS DEVELOPING YOUR OWN SELF.**

Natalie Portman

**MY MOM SAID TO ME,
'YOU KNOW, SWEETHEART,
YOU SHOULD SETTLE DOWN
AND MARRY A RICH MAN.'
I SAID, 'MOM, I AM A RICH MAN.'**

Cher

# YOU MUST LOVE AND CARE FOR YOURSELF BECAUSE THAT'S WHEN THE BEST COMES OUT.

Tina Turner

**YOU ARE ENOUGH.
BE PROUD OF
THE PERSON YOU
ARE BECOMING.**

**Tara Westover**

# YOU HAVE THE FREEDOM TO PULL THE SUPERSTAR OUT OF YOURSELF THAT YOU WERE BORN TO BE. WE WERE ALL BORN SUPERSTARS.

Lady Gaga

LUCKILY AND UNFORTUNATELY,
THERE IS NO SUPERIOR AUTHORITY
IN THIS WORLD GIVING US
PERMISSION TO BE OURSELVES
AND TO STEP FORWARD TO CHANGE
THE WORLD. IF I [HAD] WAITED FOR
PERMISSION FROM OTHERS TO
TAKE MY STAND, I WOULD STILL BE
WAITING FOR THAT PERMISSION.
THIS IS WHY MY KEY ADVICE TO YOU
TODAY IS NOT ACTUALLY ADVICE,
BUT A TASK. STOP BEING AFRAID.

Sanna Marin

OUR LIMITATIONS BECOME
OUR CHALLENGES AND THERE
IS NOTHING LIKE A CHALLENGE
TO KEEP YOU WORKING,
STRIVING, AND PUSHING FOR
MORE. EVERY DEMEANING
ROLE I WAS OFFERED, EVERY
REJECTION I WAS HANDED,
AND EVERY TIME SOMEONE
UNDERESTIMATED ME,
I FOUND ENERGY AND
RENEWED MOTIVATION.

**Michelle Yeoh**

# WE ALL HAVE THE CONFIDENCE IN US TO TAKE CHANCES AND BET ON OURSELVES.

Beyoncé

**YOU NEVER KNOW
WHAT YOU CAN
DO UNTIL YOU
HAVE TO DO IT.**

**Betty Ford**

# I STILL WANT WHAT I'VE ALWAYS WANTED ...

# TO BE THE BEST PERSON I CAN BE.

**Oprah Winfrey**

# I AM WOMAN, HEAR ME ROAR.

Helen Reddy

**NO MATTER WHO I'M WITH, I'M ALWAYS STILL DOING MY OWN THING. I'M DEFINITELY ON MY OWN PATH AND I LOVE THE IDEA OF HONOURING THAT.**

Lana Del Rey

# I NEVER INTENDED TO BECOME A RUN-OF-THE-MILL PERSON.

Barbara Jordan

# TALENT IS LIKE ELECTRICITY. WE DON'T UNDERSTAND ELECTRICITY, WE USE IT.

Maya Angelou

# I'M DA BOMB NOW, BABE!

Fantasia Barrino

**I SCORCHED
THE EARTH WITH MY
TALENT AND I LET
MY LIGHT SHINE.**

André Leon Talley

**IF THERE IS SOMETHING THAT YOU FEEL IS GOOD, SOMETHING YOU WANT TO DO, SOMETHING THAT MEANS SOMETHING TO YOU: TRY TO DO IT.**

Stan Lee

**LIFE IS SO SHORT THAT YOU CAN'T WASTE EVEN A DAY SUBSCRIBING TO WHAT SOMEONE THINKS YOU CAN DO, VERSUS KNOWING WHAT YOU CAN DO.**

Virgil Abloh

CREATIVELY, WHEN YOU PUT
YOURSELF IN UNCOMFORTABLE
MOMENTS YOU FIND OUT A
LOT ABOUT YOURSELF, AND
USUALLY YOU FIND OUT THAT
YOU'RE CAPABLE OF RISING TO
THAT BAR THAT'S SET BY THAT
UNCOMFORTABLE SITUATION.

J. Cole

IT'S IMPORTANT TO FIND YOUR
VOICE AMONGST THAT NOISE
AND TO EXPRESS IT TO THE
WORLD WITH COMPASSION
AND PASSION AND I'M REALLY
PROUD OF ANYONE WHO'S
NOT AFRAID TO DO THAT.

**Connor Franta**

# I DID MY BEST, AS I ALWAYS HAD DONE, IN SPITE OF CRUELTY AND INJUSTICE.

Anna Sewell

**I'M NOT GOING TO LIMIT MYSELF JUST BECAUSE PEOPLE WON'T ACCEPT THE FACT THAT I CAN DO SOMETHING ELSE.**

**Dolly Parton**

THE ONLY DIFFERENCE
BETWEEN BEING A WOMAN
AND BEING AN AWESOME
WOMAN LIES IN HOW YOU
DEFINE YOURSELF AND
HOW YOU CHOOSE TO
LIVE YOUR LIFE. IF YOU
BELIEVE YOURSELF TO BE
AWESOME, YOU CAN BE.

Shonda Rhimes

YOU CAN MAKE A DIFFERENCE IF YOU COME TOGETHER WITH ONE GOAL IN MIND – AND IF YOU DON'T CARE WHAT PEOPLE THINK ABOUT YOU.

Jody Williams

I RAN AND RAN AND RAN
EVERY DAY, AND I ACQUIRED
THIS SENSE OF DETERMINATION,
THIS SENSE OF SPIRIT THAT
I WOULD NEVER, NEVER
GIVE UP, NO MATTER WHAT
ELSE HAPPENED.

**Wilma Rudolph**

# I'VE ALWAYS BEEN LIKE THAT; I GIVE 100 PER CENT. I CAN'T DO IT ANY OTHER WAY.

Emma Watson

# DON'T SAVE YOUR BEST FOR WHEN YOU THINK THE MATERIAL CALLS FOR IT. ALWAYS BRING YOUR FULL POTENTIAL TO EVERY TAKE.

Gabrielle Union

# THE IMPORTANT THING IS NOT WHAT THEY THINK OF ME, BUT WHAT I THINK OF THEM.

Queen Victoria

# SELF-TRUST IS THE FIRST SECRET OF SUCCESS.

Ralph Waldo Emerson

A BIG THING THAT
CHANGED MY MUSIC WAS
CONFIDENCE. I THINK I HAD
THINGS IN MY MIND THAT
I WANTED TO ACCOMPLISH.

**Drake**

I'M PROUD THAT I'M PART OF A COMMUNITY THAT ACCEPTS ALL PEOPLE NO MATTER WHAT. I'M PROUD THAT WE'D RATHER DANCE THAN FIGHT. I'M PROUD THAT WE'D RATHER LOVE THAN HATE.

**Keegan Hirst**

COMPETE EACH DAY WITH YOU.
LOOKING AT THE LIVES OF
OTHERS CAN BE INTERESTING
BUT CAN ALSO SEVERELY
EAT AWAY AT SELF-WORTH.
BE YOUR BEST YOU. DON'T GET
HUNG UP ON WHAT SOMEONE
ELSE 'HAS' OR 'DOES'. USE
THAT ENERGY FOR YOU.

**John Cena**

YES, IT IS A VICTORY FOR
ME TO WIN THE IDITAROD.
BUT IT ISN'T AMAZING
THAT I, A WOMAN, DID
IT. I DID IT BECAUSE I AM
CAPABLE, AND WOMEN
ARE CAPABLE.

Susan Butcher

**POWER HAS TO COME FROM INSIDE. IT HAS TO COME FROM KNOWING WHO YOU ARE, WHY YOU'RE ON EARTH, WHAT IS THE MEANING OF YOUR LIFE. THAT'S POWER.**

Jane Fonda

**TWO THINGS FILL THE MIND
WITH EVER-INCREASING
WONDER AND AWE: [...]
THE STARRY HEAVENS
ABOVE ME AND THE
MORAL LAW WITHIN ME.**

Immanuel Kant

# WINNING IT ONCE CAN BE A FLUKE. WINNING IT TWICE PROVES YOU ARE THE BEST.

Althea Gibson

# IMPOSSIBLE IS NOT A FACT. IT'S AN OPINION.

# IMPOSSIBLE IS NOT A DECLARATION. IT'S A DARE.

# IMPOSSIBLE IS POTENTIAL.

# IMPOSSIBLE IS TEMPORARY.

# IMPOSSIBLE IS NOTHING.

**Muhammad Ali**

ACT UP—BE MISBEHAVED.
BUCK THE SYSTEM. FIGHT FOR
WHAT YOU BELIEVE IN. THIS IS
THE TIME TO DO IT. YOU'RE THE
ONES TO DO IT. YOUR WORLD,
LIKE NO OTHER GENERATION,
YOU ACTUALLY GET TO CREATE
THE WORLD THAT YOU CAN
IMAGINE. AND NEVER IN THE
HISTORY OF MANKIND HAS IT
BEEN SO AVAILABLE TO SO MANY
PEOPLE TO DO THAT THING.

**Mark Ruffalo**

YOU AND YOU ALONE ARE
THE ONLY PERSON THAT CAN
LIVE THE LIFE THAT WRITES
THE STORY THAT YOU WERE
MEANT TO TELL. AND THE
WORLD NEEDS YOUR STORY
BECAUSE THE WORLD NEEDS
YOUR VOICE. EVERY SINGLE
ONE OF YOU.

**Kerry Washington**

# IF I HAVE DONE ANYTHING, EVEN A LITTLE, TO HELP SMALL CHILDREN ENJOY HONEST, SIMPLE PLEASURES, I HAVE DONE A BIT OF GOOD.

Beatrix Potter

I WEAR MY
EMPOWERMENT
AT ALL TIMES.

**Miley Cyrus**

# I'M GOING
# TO LIVE
# UNTIL
# 105 ...

# AND I'M GOING TO SHOW MY THIGHS EVERY DAY.

Lena Dunham

**MY PARENTS MADE ME THINK
I WAS A GENIUS SUPERMODEL
AND IT WAS KIND OF TOO
LATE WHEN I FOUND OUT THAT
THEY HAD BEEN LYING.**

**Amy Schumer**

# YOU HAVE TO STAND UP AND SAY, 'THERE'S NOTHING WRONG WITH ME OR MY SHAPE OR WHO I AM, YOU'RE THE ONE WITH THE PROBLEM!'

Jennifer Lopez

# MY BODY IS SOMETHING THAT I WILL NEVER APOLOGISE FOR. MY BODY WILL CONSTANTLY GO THROUGH CHANGE. AND SO WILL YOURS. AND THAT'S FINE.

Lili Reinhart

I DON'T WANT TO BE AN 'AGELESS BEAUTY'. I WANT TO BE A WOMAN WHO IS THE BEST I CAN BE AT MY AGE.

**Sharon Stone**

EVEN ON *AMERICAN IDOL* I WAS
REALLY THIN, BUT I WAS BIGGER
THAN THE OTHER GIRLS ON THE
SHOW, SO PEOPLE WOULD SAY
THINGS TO ME. BUT LUCKILY, I AM
SUPER CONFIDENT, SO I'VE NEVER
HAD A PROBLEM WITH SHUTTING
PEOPLE DOWN AND SAYING,
'YEAH, YOU KNOW, THAT'S JUST
WHAT I'M ROCKING. IT'S FINE.'

Kelly Clarkson

I WOULD SAY TO ANY YOUNG
WOMAN, YOU'RE BEING LIED
TO. WHO IS MAKING MONEY
OFF THIS? YOU'RE BEING LIED
TO AND YOU'RE BEING TRICKED
OFF YOUR PATH... YOU'VE GOT
AWESOME THINGS COMING
YOUR WAY. JUST STAY ON YOUR
PATH AND JUST RIDE IT OUT.

**Justine Bateman**

# I AM PERFECT
# THE WAY I AM
# RIGHT NOW.

Wendy Williams

# I'VE ALWAYS BEEN KNOWN FOR MY BOOBS, BUT IT PISSES ME OFF, BECAUSE I DO ALSO HAVE A GREAT ASS.

Sofía Vergara

# YOU CAN'T SIT AROUND AND WAIT FOR SOMEBODY TO SAY WHO YOU ARE. YOU NEED TO WRITE IT AND PAINT IT AND DO IT.

Faith Ringgold

**I'M VERY AMBITIOUS.
BUT I UNDERSTAND THAT YOU
CAN'T DO – ACTUALLY, I TAKE
THAT BACK BECAUSE I DON'T
BELIEVE IN THE WORD *CAN'T*.**

**Lewis Hamilton**

SOMETIMES, I FEEL
DISCRIMINATED AGAINST,
BUT IT DOES NOT MAKE
ME ANGRY. IT MERELY
ASTONISHES ME. HOW CAN
ANY DENY THEMSELVES
THE PLEASURE OF MY
COMPANY? IT'S BEYOND ME.

**Zora Neale Hurston**

I'M COMPETITIVE, IN THE
SENSE THAT I WANT TO WORK
HARD AND I TRY TO NOT BE
COMPETITIVE WITH ANYONE
ELSE. I TRY TO JUST BE LIKE,
'I ALREADY DID THAT, OK,
SO NOW I GOT TO DO BETTER.'

**Zendaya**

# YEAH, WELL. I DON'T TRY TO BE AWESOME. IT JUST COMES NATURAL.

Rick Riordan

IF I WAIT FOR SOMEONE ELSE
TO VALIDATE MY EXISTENCE,
IT WILL MEAN THAT I'M
SHORT-CHANGING MYSELF.

**Zanele Muholi**

**LOVE YOURSELF FIRST AND EVERYTHING ELSE FALLS INTO LINE. YOU REALLY HAVE TO LOVE YOURSELF TO GET ANYTHING DONE IN THIS WORLD.**

Lucille Ball

I FEEL LIKE I'M BECOMING A PERSON I REALLY LOVE AND DOING THINGS I FEEL REALLY PROUD OF. IN MANY WAYS IN MY LIFE, I FEEL LIKE I'M JUST NOW WAKING UP.

Billie Eilish

# I DON'T HAVE ANYTHING TO SAY I'M SORRY FOR.

Jennifer Lawrence

# I WANT TO BUILD MY EMPIRE. IN MY FIELD, I HAVE ALWAYS SEEN MEN DO IT [...] NOW, IT'S A WOMAN'S TURN.

**Nicki Minaj**

A WINNER IS SOMEONE WHO RECOGNISES HIS GOD-GIVEN TALENTS, WORKS HIS TAIL OFF TO DEVELOP THEM INTO SKILLS, AND USES THESE SKILLS TO ACCOMPLISH HIS GOALS.

Larry Bird

**NOTHING BEATS THE JOY OF BEING ABLE TO EXPRESS YOURSELF FREELY. EVERYONE SHOULD EMBRACE THAT PRECIOUS MINDSET OF NOT CARING ABOUT WHAT OTHERS THINK.**

Arthur Arbesser

# I WAS STRONG. I WAS BRAVE.

# NOTHING COULD VANQUISH ME.

Cheryl Strayed

I HAVE ALWAYS
BEEN DEEPLY, DEEPLY
CONFIDENT IN MY CHOICES
AND IN WHO I AM.

**Willie Norris**

# I WANT TO BE WORTHY OF RESPECT BECAUSE I EXCEL AT WHAT I DO. CLASSY – THAT'S HOW I WANT TO BE DEFINED. A CLASS ACT.

Hilary Lindh

I AM NOW GETTING
INTO THIS GROOVE IN
MY CAREER WHERE
I KNOW WHAT I CAN
TAKE, WHAT I CAN GIVE,
AND WHAT I WILL NOT
ACCEPT ANYMORE.

**Florence Pugh**

I'VE NEVER FELT MORE POWERFUL. I FEEL MORE HONEST. I FEEL LIKE I'M NOT PRETENDING ...

# I FEEL LIKE I'M EMBRACING RIGHT WHERE I AM. I FEEL REALLY COMFORTABLE.

**Andie MacDowell**

**YOU ARE THE LOVELIEST, TENDEREST, AND MOST BEAUTIFUL PERSON I HAVE EVER KNOWN – AND EVEN THAT IS AN UNDERSTATEMENT.**

F. Scott Fitzgerald,
to wife Zelda Fitzgerald

# I'D LIKE TO TAKE OVER THE WORLD ... IF I COULD.

**Dua Lipa**

# I'M NEVER AFRAID TO TRY ANYTHING.

Hailey Bieber

I FEEL SO PROUD
OF THE WOMAN
THAT I'VE BECOME.

**Paris Hilton**

**I STAND BY EVERY MISTAKE I'VE EVER MADE. SO JUDGE AWAY.**

Kristen Stewart

# BE YOU, THAT'S IT.

Jon Batiste

Quadrille, Penguin Random House UK,
One Embassy Gardens, 8 Viaduct
Gardens, London SW11 7BW

Quadrille Publishing Limited
is part of the Penguin Random House
group of companies whose
addresses can be found at
global.penguinrandomhouse.com

Penguin
Random House
UK

Published by Quadrille in 2024

www.penguin.co.uk

A CIP catalogue record for this book
is available from the British Library

ISBN 9781784887216
10 9 8 7 6 5 4 3 2 1

Publishing Director: Kajal Mistry
Editorial Director: Judith Hannam
Senior Commissioning Editor:
Kate Burkett
Text curated by: Satu Fox
Editorial Assistant: Harriet Thornley
Design: Claire Warner Studio
Production Controller: Gary Hayes

Colour reproduction by p2d

Printed in China by RR Donnelley Asia
Printing Solution Limited

The authorised representative in
the EEA is Penguin Random House
Ireland, Morrison Chambers,
32 Nassau Street, Dublin D02 YH68.

MIX
Paper | Supporting
responsible forestry
FSC® C018179

Penguin Random House is committed
to a sustainable future for our
business, our readers and our planet.
This book is made from Forest
Stewardship Council® certified paper.